EMBRACE THE MESS

A Journey through Love, Loss and Trans

Violet Bonner

Table of contents

INTRODUCTION

Life is a fascinating journey, often characterized by unpredictability, chaos, and unexpected encounters. It's a story of twists and turns, filled with moments that can transform the mundane into the extraordinary. Two such aspects of life that we'll explore in this piece are 'The Catalyst of a CVS Parking Lot' and 'The Power of Embracing Life's Messiness.'

These seemingly unrelated topics converge to reveal a profound truth: the most beautiful and transformative experiences often emerge from the messiest, most unexpected corners of our lives.

The Catalyst of a CVS Parking Lot

Imagine a mundane evening, with the sun setting in hues of orange and pink, casting long shadows across a nondescript CVS pharmacy parking lot. The scene seems ordinary, almost banal, yet it serves as a vivid illustration of life's unpredictability and its potential to bring extraordinary moments.

In the aisles of the pharmacy, people bustle about, their minds preoccupied with shopping lists, prescriptions, and the rush of daily life. But amidst this ordinary backdrop, a chance encounter unfolds. Two strangers, brought together by fate in this unassuming parking lot, share a brief but profound connection.

Perhaps they exchange a few words, maybe a smile, or perhaps they merely make eye contact that sparks something within them. In that fleeting moment, the world pauses, and the CVS parking lot is transformed into a stage where the ordinary becomes extraordinary. It's a reminder that life's most remarkable moments can happen anywhere, even in the most unexpected places.

The CVS parking lot, in this context, represents the idea that life's catalysts are often hidden in plain sight. They can be found in the ordinary places we frequent, waiting for us to recognize them. This story reminds us to be open to serendipity, to embrace the beauty of the unexpected, and to cherish those seemingly inconsequential moments that can change our lives forever.

The Power of Embracing Life's Messiness

Life is far from linear; it's an intricate tapestry woven with threads of joy, sorrow, success, failure, love, and heartbreak. It's a masterpiece of chaos and messiness, and it's in this very messiness that the true power of life resides.

When we attempt to control every aspect of our lives, to neatly arrange everything into predefined boxes, we risk missing out on the raw, unfiltered beauty that comes from embracing the chaos. Life's messiness is a testament to its authenticity, a reminder that perfection is an illusion.

Consider some of your most treasured memories. Were they meticulously planned, or did they emerge unexpectedly from the messiness of life? It's often in the unplanned, imperfect, and messy moments that we find the most profound experiences and learn the most about ourselves.

The power of embracing life's messiness lies in the freedom it grants us to be human. It allows us to make mistakes, to take risks, and to grow from the challenges we face. It encourages us to let go of the need for control and perfection and instead surrender to the beautiful chaos of existence.

Life's magic lies in its ability to surprise us, to challenge us, and to take us on a journey filled with unexpected twists and turns. The CVS parking lot represents the unexpected catalysts that can change the course of our lives, and the power of embracing life's messiness reminds us to find beauty in imperfection.

So, as you navigate the ups and downs of life, remember that some of the most incredible stories are born from the messiest moments, and some of the most profound connections are forged in the most unlikely places. Embrace the chaos, and let life's unpredictability lead you to the extraordinary.

CHAPTER 1

Facing Life's Turmoil

Love, Loss, and Unexpected Turns

Love, the emotion that fuels our hearts and inspires our souls, is a force of nature. It sweeps us off our feet, fills our days with warmth, and paints our world in the brightest of hues. But love is also a journey fraught with twists and turns, where joy and sorrow walk hand in hand. It's a journey that often leads us through the labyrinthine paths of loss and unexpected turns.

In the beginning, love is a flame that burns brilliantly, casting aside the shadows of doubt and fear. It's a dance of two souls finding their rhythm, their harmonious cadence in the symphony of life. Love blossoms like a fragile flower, delicate and beautiful, and we tend to it with care, nurturing its growth. But life has a way of throwing curveballs, leading us down roads we never imagined we'd travel.

Loss, the bitter companion of love, is an inevitable part of the human experience. It can come in many forms: the loss of a loved one, the loss of a relationship, or the loss of a dream. Each loss leaves a void, a gaping wound in our hearts that seems impossible to heal. It's in these moments of grief and despair that we discover the true depth of our love. We mourn the absence of what was, but in that sorrow, we find the essence of what remains.

Unexpected turns, like sharp bends in the road, force us to reevaluate our course. Life is a journey full of surprises, some delightful and others challenging. These unexpected twists can lead us away from the path we once envisioned, but they can also open new doors and unveil hidden opportunities. It's during these moments of uncertainty that love becomes our guiding star, illuminating the darkness and providing a sense of purpose.

Love has the power to transform loss into resilience. It teaches us that even when we lose something dear, we gain a deeper understanding of ourselves and the world around us. It reminds us that unexpected turns can lead to unforeseen destinations, filled with unexpected joys and discoveries.

Love, loss, and unexpected turns are the threads that weave the tapestry of our lives. They are interconnected, interdependent, and inextricable. Without love, loss would hold no meaning; without loss, we would not fully appreciate the depths of love. And without unexpected turns, life would lack the element of surprise and adventure that keeps us on our toes.

So, as we navigate the rollercoaster of life, let us cherish the love we have, even as we acknowledge the inevitability of loss and the unpredictability of the road ahead. Let us remember that love, in all its forms, is a precious gift that can help us navigate even the darkest of times. And let us embrace the unexpected turns, for they may lead us to the most extraordinary destinations we could ever imagine.

Pivoting Amidst a Pandemic

The COVID-19 pandemic, an unprecedented global crisis, brought with it a multitude of challenges and disruptions that have reshaped our lives in profound ways. From the sudden shift to remote work and online education to the closure of businesses and the suspension of travel, individuals and organizations across the world have been forced to adapt and pivot in response to the ever-evolving circumstances. Pivoting amidst a pandemic has been both a survival imperative and an opportunity for growth and innovation.

Adapting to Remote Work: One of the most significant changes brought about by the pandemic was the widespread adoption of remote work. Companies had to quickly pivot from traditional office setups to remote work environments. This transition demanded a rethinking of processes, communication, and collaboration. While challenges such as isolation and work-life balance arose, it also showcased the potential for flexibility and the ability to leverage technology in new and efficient ways.

E-commerce and Digital Transformation: With physical stores closing and consumer behavior shifting online, businesses had to accelerate their digital transformation efforts. Small retailers and local businesses pivoted to e-commerce, and even industries like healthcare and education embraced telemedicine and virtual learning. This digital pivot not only ensured survival but also opened up new avenues for reaching customers and clients.

Innovation and Creativity: The pandemic forced individuals and organizations to think outside the box. Creative solutions emerged, such as the rapid development of vaccines, the use of 3D printing for manufacturing personal protective equipment (PPE), and the transformation of event planning into virtual experiences. These innovations demonstrated the power of human adaptability and the capacity to pivot in the face of adversity.

Health and Well-being: The pandemic underscored the importance of health and well-being. People pivoted toward healthier lifestyles, focusing on physical fitness and mental health. Employers began to prioritize employee well-being by offering flexible work hours, mental health support, and more comprehensive benefits. The pandemic served as a catalyst for recognizing the need for a healthier work-life balance.

Community and Solidarity: Amidst the isolation caused by lockdowns and social distancing, communities came together in unprecedented ways. Neighbors helped one another with grocery shopping, and countless volunteers stepped up to support vulnerable populations. This spirit of solidarity demonstrated humanity's resilience and the power of community in the face of adversity.

Environmental Impact: The pandemic also led to a pivot in environmental consciousness. As travel restrictions reduced pollution and carbon emissions, individuals and organizations alike began to reevaluate their environmental impact. Sustainability and eco-conscious practices gained momentum, paving the way for a greener future.

Pivoting amidst a pandemic has not been without its share of difficulties. The uncertainty and the need to adapt rapidly have challenged us in profound ways. However, it has also shown our resilience, creativity, and adaptability as individuals and as a society.

As we continue to navigate the ongoing challenges posed by the pandemic, let us not forget the lessons we have learned. Let us carry forward the spirit of innovation, the importance of community, and the recognition of the need for flexibility in our personal and professional lives.

CHAPTER 2

Breaking down Barriers

The Facade of Strength

In a world that often equates strength with unwavering resilience and an impenetrable exterior, I had mastered the art of wearing a facade. It was a mask of invincibility, a shield I meticulously crafted to protect myself from the vulnerabilities that lay beneath the surface.

I believed that strength meant never letting anyone see my weaknesses, never admitting to moments of doubt, and never allowing emotions to creep through the armor I had built.

This facade served me well—or so I thought. It allowed me to navigate the challenges of life, to push forward when faced with adversity, and to project an image of unwavering confidence. But beneath it all, there was a growing hollowness, a sense of disconnect from my own emotions and the genuine connections with others. I had built walls around my heart, and though they kept me safe, they also kept me isolated.

The Day I Let My Guard Down

There comes a moment in everyone's life when the facade begins to crack. For me, that moment arrived unexpectedly, like a bolt of lightning on a clear day. It was a seemingly ordinary afternoon, and I found myself overwhelmed by a series of personal and professional setbacks that left me feeling utterly defeated. The weight of it all became too much to bear, and the cracks in my carefully constructed facade began to show.

I remember sitting alone in my dimly lit room, tears streaming down my face, and a torrent of emotions flooding over me. It was in that moment of despair that I realized the futility of my facade. The strength I had portrayed to the world was a brittle shell, and it was shattering, leaving me exposed and raw. It was a humbling, frightening, and yet strangely liberating moment.

As I sat there, vulnerable and broken, something remarkable happened. Instead of feeling weaker, I felt a strange sense of strength in my vulnerability. It was as if I had finally allowed myself to be human, to acknowledge my imperfections, and to reach out for help and support from those around me. I discovered that true strength was not in pretending to be invincible but in embracing our vulnerability, for it is in our vulnerability that we find our common humanity.

In the days that followed, I began to dismantle the walls I had built around my heart. I started sharing my fears, doubts, and insecurities with trusted friends and loved ones. To my surprise, they didn't see me as weaker; they saw me as authentic, relatable, and brave for letting down my guard.

This chapter is a testament to the transformative power of vulnerability. It is a journey of self-discovery, a journey from the facade of strength to the authenticity of vulnerability. It's a journey that teaches us that true strength lies not in the absence of weaknesses but in our ability to acknowledge and embrace them.

In doing so, we break down the barriers that keep us isolated and discover the healing touch of vulnerability that connects us to others in a profound and meaningful way.

CHAPTER 3

The Question That Altered Everything

Why We Dodge Our Emotions?

Emotions are the essence of human experience, yet we often go to great lengths to avoid them. We sidestep sadness, suppress anger, and numb ourselves to fear, all in an attempt to maintain a facade of control and composure. But why do we dodge our emotions?

The answer lies in our societal conditioning. From an early age, we're told to be strong, to hide our vulnerabilities, and to not burden others with our feelings. We learn that emotions are a sign of weakness, something to be ashamed of. So, we create intricate defense mechanisms to protect ourselves from the discomfort of facing our emotions head-on.

But here's the paradox: the more we avoid our emotions, the more they control us. They fester beneath the surface, manifesting as anxiety, depression, or even physical ailments. It's a ticking time bomb, and it's only a matter of time before it explodes. That's when we're forced to ask the question that alters everything.

The Healing Potential of Grief

Grief is a natural response to loss, whether it's the death of a loved one, the end of a relationship, or the loss of a dream. Yet, it's an emotion we often suppress or rush through in our quest to "move on." In doing so, we miss out on the healing potential of grief.

Grief is not just about sadness; it's a complex emotional process that allows us to honor what we've lost. It's a journey that demands our attention, inviting us to reflect on the depth of our connections and the significance of what we've experienced. By allowing ourselves to grieve fully, we open the door to profound healing and transformation.

Uncovering Emotions Hidden in Plain Sight

Emotions aren't always obvious. Sometimes, they lurk beneath the surface, camouflaged by the busyness of our lives and the distractions we use to avoid them. It's easy to ignore these emotions hidden in plain sight, but doing so comes at a cost.

By becoming detectives of our own emotional landscapes, we gain insight into our true selves. We learn to decipher the subtle signals our bodies and minds send us and, in doing so, we embark on a profound journey of self-discovery.

What am I feeling and why?

In the grand theater of life, where our thoughts and emotions dance in intricate patterns, there exists a simple yet profound question that has the power to disrupt the status quo, alter our course, and ignite the spark of transformation: "What am I feeling, and why?"

Throughout our existence, we are constantly bombarded by external stimuli, and our minds are abuzz with thoughts, desires, and distractions. In the hustle and bustle of daily life, it's easy to lose touch with our inner selves, to overlook the emotions that course through our veins like an invisible river. We often brush our feelings aside, suppress them, or simply let them simmer beneath the surface, unexamined and unacknowledged.

But what if we paused for a moment? What if we took a step back from the chaos and cacophony of the outside world and turned our gaze inward, toward the ever-shifting landscape of our emotions? What if we dared to probe our own emotions by asking, "What am I feeling, and why?"

This deceptively simple question holds the key to unlocking a deeper understanding of ourselves and the world around us. It is an invitation to explore the rich tapestry of our emotional lives, to peel back the layers of our consciousness, and to uncover the hidden motivations and fears that drive our actions.

To ask "What am I feeling, and why?" is to embark on a journey of self-discovery and self-acceptance. It is an act of courage, for it requires us to confront the raw and sometimes uncomfortable truths that lie within us. It demands that we let go of the armor we wear to shield ourselves from vulnerability and instead embrace the vulnerability as a source of strength.

When we take the time to honestly answer this question, we open the door to a profound transformation. We gain insight into the patterns that govern our behavior, the beliefs that shape our perceptions, and the wounds that continue to haunt us. We begin to see the interplay between our thoughts and emotions, recognizing that our feelings are not arbitrary but often rooted in our deeply held beliefs and past experiences.

Moreover, asking "What am I feeling, and why?" is a powerful tool for navigating the complexities of human relationships. It allows us to empathize with others, to understand their motivations, and to build deeper connections based on genuine understanding. By tuning into our own emotions, we become better equipped to navigate the emotional landscapes of those around us, fostering empathy and compassion.

But this question is not just about self-exploration or interpersonal relationships; it has far-reaching implications for our overall well-being and happiness. When we confront our feelings and understand their origins, we can make more informed decisions about how to respond to them. We can choose to let go of toxic emotions that no longer serve us and cultivate positive ones that bring us joy and fulfillment.

So, dear reader, I invite you to embark on this transformative journey with an open heart and a curious mind. "What am I feeling, and why?" is a good question to ask oneself. Make this query your compass, using it to lead you toward a better comprehension of both yourself and the environment you live in. In doing so, you may discover that the power to change your life lies not in external circumstances but within the depths of your own heart and mind.

Confronting the emotions we've been dodging, embracing the healing potential of grief, and becoming adept at uncovering the hidden emotions that shape our lives. It's a chapter that challenges us to ask the question that can truly alter everything: "What am I feeling, and why?"

CHAPTER 4

Embracing the Beautiful Chaos

The Multitude of Grief's Colors

Grief is not a one-dimensional emotion; it's a spectrum of colors that paint our experience of loss. At first glance, grief may appear as a monochrome canvas, overwhelmed by the darkness of sorrow. However, if we look closely, we'll find a vast array of emotions intertwined in this intricate tapestry.

The deep indigos of despair may seem overwhelming, but they remind us of the depth of our love for what or whom we've lost. The fiery reds of anger can be disorienting, yet they signal our unwillingness to accept injustice or a cruel twist of fate. Earthy browns of nostalgia bring warmth, as we cherish the memories that remain etched in our hearts. And the fragile pastels of acceptance gently whisper that healing is possible.

Grief compels us to reevaluate our priorities, to find meaning in the seemingly insignificant, and to seek solace in the most unexpected places. In the midst of chaos, we find wisdom, and in the depths of despair, we discover the resilience of the human spirit.

CHAPTER 5

Navigating Life's Upside-Downs

Dissolving Relationships: Rediscovering Love

Relationships are intricate, multifaceted bonds that often evolve over time. The journey of love can be both beautiful and challenging, as individuals and couples navigate the twists and turns of life together. One common theme in many relationships is change, and sometimes, this change leads to the dissolution of the relationship itself. However, even in the aftermath of a breakup or a strained connection, there is the potential for rediscovering love – not just with another person but with oneself.

The Dissolution of Relationships:

The dissolution of a relationship can be emotionally overwhelming. Whether it's the end of a romantic partnership, the distancing of friends, or the breakdown of

In navigating grief, it's important to acknowledge and embrace this spectrum of emotions. Healing doesn't mean moving from darkness to light but learning to coexist with the many shades of grief. Each color has its own significance, its role in the process of mourning. Just as an artist uses a diverse palette to create a masterpiece, so too do these emotions contribute to the richness and complexity of our journey through grief.

Humor in the Darkest Hours

Amid the somber depths of grief, humor can be an unexpected visitor. It's not about making light of our pain but finding moments of respite and connection amidst the darkness. Laughter, even in the face of profound loss, is a testament to the resilience of the human spirit.

Humor emerges from shared memories, funny anecdotes, and even moments of absurdity. These instances are not disrespectful to the gravity of our loss but rather affirm our capacity to find joy in unexpected places. They offer a breath of fresh air, a temporary release from the relentless sadness that can accompany grief.

Recognizing and appreciating the humor that occasionally graces our grief can be a powerful coping mechanism. It reminds us that even in our darkest hours, we have the capacity to find moments of lightness, camaraderie, and even hope. Laughter is a universal language that binds us together, a reminder that, despite our pain, life continues to offer moments of connection and joy.

Lessons from the Incongruous Moments

Grief is a perplexing teacher, often imparting its most profound lessons in the most unexpected places. It's as if the chaos of grief nudges us toward moments of clarity and insight. In our deepest sorrow, we may discover a newfound appreciation for life's fleeting beauty.

These incongruous moments may appear in the mundane routines of daily life, in the faces of strangers who offer unexpected kindness, or in the simple beauty of a sunset. Grief teaches us the value of empathy, urging us to reach out to others who are suffering. It underscores the importance of cherishing our relationships, as they provide solace in our times of need.

family ties, it's a process that often brings grief, sadness, and even anger. The reasons for relationship dissolution can vary widely, from personal growth and changing priorities to conflicts and betrayals. No matter the cause, the feelings of loss are real and valid.

Rediscovering Love Within

In the aftermath of a relationship's dissolution, there's an opportunity for profound personal growth. This process begins with self-reflection and self-love. You must first love yourself in order to love someone else. Take time to understand who you are as an individual, your values, your desires, and your dreams. Reconnect with your passions and interests that may have been set aside during the relationship.

Practicing self-compassion is essential during this phase. Understand that healing takes time, and it's okay to feel pain, anger, or sadness. Seek support from friends, family, or a therapist to help process these emotions and gain perspective on the situation.

Learning from the Past

Every relationship teaches us valuable lessons. Even in the pain of dissolution, there are insights to be gained. Reflect on what worked and what didn't in the previous relationship. Consider how you can use these insights to make healthier choices in future connections.

Forgiving and Letting Go

To rediscover love, it's crucial to forgive not only the other person but also yourself. Forgiveness doesn't mean condoning past actions or pretending they didn't hurt. It means acknowledging the pain and choosing to release the emotional burden. Holding onto grudges and resentments only prolongs the healing process.

Opening Up to New Possibilities

As you heal and rediscover yourself, you'll be better prepared to open your heart to new relationships. It's essential to enter new connections with an open mind and heart, free from the baggage of past relationships. Each person and relationship is unique, and the future holds the potential for profound love and connection.

Job Loss and Career Crossroads

Job loss is a life-altering event that can shake one's sense of security and stability. It often propels individuals into a career crossroads, forcing them to reevaluate their professional goals and direction. While this transition can be daunting, it also offers an opportunity for personal and career growth, a chance to rediscover one's passions, and chart a new and fulfilling course.

The Emotional Impact of Job Loss

Losing a job can bring forth a whirlwind of emotions—shock, anger, sadness, and anxiety. Love yourself first, then love someone else. Instead of repressing these emotions, it's important to recognize and deal with them. Must respect oneself Support from friends, family, or a therapist can provide a safe space to express your emotions and gain perspective.

Assessing Your Skills and Interests

Job loss can serve as a catalyst for self-discovery. Consider evaluating your values, interests, and talents. What are you truly passionate about? What talents do you possess? Understanding these aspects can help you explore new career possibilities that align with your passions.

Exploring Career Options

At the career crossroads, it's an opportunity to explore various career options. Consider what you've always wanted to do but never had the chance. Research different industries, take courses, or attend networking events to gain insight into new fields. Additionally, think about getting advice from professional counselors or mentors who may offer insightful advice. Reskilling and Upskilling:

In a rapidly evolving job market, reskilling and upskilling are critical. Invest in learning new talents or developing ones you already have. Online courses, workshops, and certifications can help you stay competitive and broaden your career prospects.

Entrepreneurship and Freelancing

Job loss can be an ideal moment to explore entrepreneurship or freelancing. If you have a business idea or a skill set that can be monetized independently, take the leap. Start small, create a business plan, and gradually build your venture.

Networking and Personal Branding

Networking is crucial when transitioning careers. Attend industry-related events, connect with professionals on LinkedIn, and join online communities. In a crowded employment market, developing a strong personal brand might help you stand out.

Financial Planning and Budgeting

Job loss can disrupt your financial stability. Create a budget to manage expenses and prioritize financial planning. Consider temporary part-time work or freelance gigs to bridge the income gap during your career transition.

Resilience and Patience

Navigating job loss and career crossroads can be challenging, but resilience is key. Understand that finding the right opportunity may take time. Maintain a positive attitude, stay persistent, and remain open to unexpected opportunities.

CHAPTER 6

Real-Life Tales and Insights

Stories from the Heart of Adversity

Unexpected setbacks are a regular occurrence in life. Sometimes, these curveballs are relentless storms, and other times they are seemingly insurmountable mountains. Yet, it's in these moments that we discover the true strength of the human spirit. Throughout history and across cultures, there are countless stories of individuals who have triumphed over adversity.

Consider the tale of Anne Frank, a young Jewish girl who, despite facing unimaginable persecution during the Holocaust, penned a diary that continues to inspire the world with its resilience and hope. Or the story of Malala Yousafzai, who defied the Taliban to advocate for girls' education and became the youngest Nobel laureate in history. These stories remind us that even in the darkest of times, the human spirit can shine brilliantly.

Lessons from Life's Unforeseen Twists

Life rarely follows a linear path, and often, our best-laid plans are disrupted by unexpected twists and turns. These unforeseen events can be disorienting and challenging, but they also provide us with valuable opportunities for growth and adaptation.

One of the most famous tales of unexpected twists is that of Steve Jobs, who was ousted from the company he co-founded, Apple, only to return years later and lead it to unprecedented success. His journey teaches us that setbacks can be stepping stones, and sometimes, the greatest innovations arise from the ashes of failure.

We will also explore the story of J.K. Rowling, a struggling single mother who turned adversity into literary magic by creating the Harry Potter series. Her experience reminds us that even in our darkest hours, we possess the power to conjure our own destinies.

Life is a journey, and along the way, we accumulate wisdom from our experiences. It's through the challenges we face, the mistakes we make, and the victories we celebrate that we gain valuable insights that shape our perspective on the world.

We'll delve into the wisdom of Nelson Mandela, who emerged from 27 years of imprisonment with a heart unburdened by hatred, leading South Africa to a peaceful transition from apartheid to democracy. His journey teaches us the transformative power of forgiveness and reconciliation.

Let us also reflect on the insights of Maya Angelou, whose poetic words and life journey inspire us to rise above adversity with grace and resilience. Her wisdom reminds us that we have the capacity to transcend our circumstances and become better versions of ourselves.

CHAPTER 7

Practices for Healing and Growth

The Art of Mindfulness

Mindfulness is a practice that invites us to be fully present in the moment, embracing each experience with open awareness and non-judgment. In a world filled with distractions and constant stimuli, mindfulness offers a sanctuary of peace and clarity.

Through mindfulness, we learn to observe our thoughts and emotions without attachment, gaining a deeper understanding of our inner landscape. This practice enables us to break free from the chains of anxiety about the future and regrets about the past, allowing us to savor the richness of the here and now.

By being attuned to our breath, sensations, and surroundings, we can reduce stress, enhance our emotional well-being, and develop greater empathy for ourselves and others. Mindfulness is a transformative tool that empowers us to respond to life's challenges with equanimity and grace.

Journaling Your Transformation

Writing has a profound therapeutic effect, serving as a bridge between our inner world and external reality. Keeping a journal is a powerful means of self-expression, self-discovery, and personal growth.

Through journaling, we can document our thoughts, emotions, and experiences, enabling us to gain insights into our patterns, desires, and fears. It serves as a safe space to explore our dreams, set goals, and track our progress on the journey of self-improvement.

Moreover, journaling can help us release pent-up emotions, untangle complex issues, and find clarity in times of confusion. It provides a tangible record of our evolution, reminding us of how far we've come and inspiring us to keep moving forward.

Human beings are inherently social creatures, and our connections with others play a pivotal role in our well-being and resilience. Building and nurturing meaningful relationships can be a source of profound healing and growth.

In times of adversity, the support of loved ones can provide solace and strength. Acts of kindness, empathy, and compassion forge bonds that can help us weather life's storms. Sharing our experiences and vulnerabilities with trusted confidants can be a cathartic release, alleviating the burden of our struggles.

The practice of connecting with diverse communities, whether through shared interests, support groups, or volunteering, can expand our perspectives, increase our resilience, and enhance our sense of purpose. As we connect with others, we discover that our stories and struggles are not isolated but woven into the tapestry of the human experience.

CHAPTER 8

Discovering Purpose amidst Disorder

Taking Stock of Life's Treasures

In the rush of our daily lives, it's easy to lose sight of the treasures that surround us. Material pursuits, societal expectations, and the pursuit of success can sometimes cloud our vision. However, discovering purpose often begins with taking a step back and appreciating the richness of our lives as they are.

This practice involves recognizing and cherishing the relationships, experiences, and moments that bring us joy, fulfillment, and a sense of meaning. By acknowledging these treasures, we gain clarity about what truly matters to us and what we want to prioritize in our journey towards purpose.

To find our purpose amidst disorder, we must engage in deep introspection. We need to question our values, aspirations, and motivations, understanding what resonates with our authentic selves. Often, our true purpose lies beneath layers of societal expectations and external influences.

By asking ourselves profound questions about our passions, the impact we want to have on the world, and the legacy we hope to leave behind, we can unearth the essence of our purpose. This process can be transformative, guiding us toward endeavors that align with our core values and resonate with our hearts.

The Art of Reinvention

Life is a continuous journey of growth and transformation, and purpose can evolve over time. The art of reinvention involves embracing change and being open to the possibility of shifting our life's purpose in response to new experiences, insights, and circumstances.

Many great individuals have discovered their purpose through reinvention. For instance, Colonel Harland

Sanders, the founder of KFC, found his purpose later in life when he turned his passion for cooking into a thriving business. His story teaches us that it's never too late to reinvent ourselves and pursue what truly matters

CHAPTER 9

Embracing True Freedom

In the pursuit of a life filled with meaning and purpose, we often find ourselves seeking freedom. We long to break free from the constraints that hold us back, whether they be external forces or internal doubts. But what is true freedom? Is it the absence of pain, the eradication of fear, or the blissful escape from messy emotions?

Liberated from Fear, Not from Pain

True freedom begins with the understanding that it is not the absence of pain that defines our liberation but the ability to confront and transcend it. Pain is an integral part of the human experience, an essential teacher that helps us grow and evolve. We cannot escape pain, nor should we strive to do so. Instead, we should embrace it as an opportunity for growth and transformation.

Fear, on the other hand, is often the root cause of our suffering. It limits our potential, paralyzes us, and keeps us trapped in a cycle of self-doubt and avoidance. True freedom is the liberation from this fear. It is the courage to face our fears head-on, to acknowledge them, and to move forward despite them. It is the realization that we can choose how we respond to fear and that we are not controlled by it.

Living Authentically with Messy Emotions

In our quest for freedom, we may also be tempted to seek an escape from our messy emotions. We might believe that true freedom means always feeling happy, content, and at peace. However, this is an unrealistic and unattainable goal. Emotions are a fundamental aspect of being human, and they come in all shades and forms. True freedom is not about avoiding or suppressing these emotions but about embracing them with compassion and authenticity.

Living authentically means acknowledging the full spectrum of our emotions, from joy and love to anger and sadness. It means allowing ourselves to feel without judgment or shame. It is through this acceptance of our emotional complexity that we can truly connect with ourselves and others. It is through our vulnerability that we find strength, and it is through our authenticity that we discover true freedom.

The Path to Self-Acceptance

At the heart of true freedom lies self-acceptance. It is the acceptance of our flaws, imperfections, and vulnerabilities that allows us to be truly free. Self-acceptance is not about complacency or resignation; it is about embracing our authentic selves and acknowledging that we are enough just as we are.

The path to self-acceptance is not always easy. It requires self-reflection, self-compassion, and a willingness to let go of self-judgment and comparison. It is a journey of self-discovery and self-love. But it is also a journey worth taking because it leads to a profound sense of freedom.

True freedom is not the absence of pain or the escape from messy emotions. It is the liberation from fear, the courage to face our emotions authentically, and the path to self-acceptance. It is a journey of self-discovery and growth that allows us to live a life filled with purpose and meaning. Embrace true freedom, and you will find that it is not a destination but a way of life.

CONCLUSION

Embracing the Path Ahead

As we conclude our exploration of life's intricate tapestry, we find ourselves standing at the precipice of an uncharted future. The journey we've undertaken, filled with its complexities, joys, sorrows, and transformations, has brought us to this moment of reflection and understanding.

Continual Embrace of Life's Complexity

Life is a complex and ever-evolving puzzle. It presents us with challenges, surprises, and intricacies that constantly test our understanding and resilience. However, it is in the embrace of this complexity that we find our greatest opportunities for growth and self-discovery.

Embracing life's complexity means acknowledging that answers are not always clear-cut, and the paths we choose may not always lead where we expect. It calls for a willingness to navigate the gray areas, to grapple with uncertainty, and to appreciate the beauty that lies within the intricacies of our existence.

Through every twist and turn, we learn that it is not the destination but the journey itself that holds the true value. Every experience, whether joyful or painful, contributes to the tapestry of our lives. It is in these moments of complexity that we find our strengths and capacities, forging our character and resilience.

The Unending Journey of Love, Loss, and Transformation

Love, loss, and transformation are the threads that weave through the fabric of our lives, shaping who we are and who we become. Love is the force that binds us to one another, providing warmth, support, and purpose. It is the light that guides us through the darkest of times and the source of our deepest joys.

Yet, love is inseparable from loss. As we traverse the terrain of existence, we inevitably encounter moments of separation, grief, and heartache. These experiences, though painful, are also transformative. They challenge us to grow, to find strength in vulnerability, and to appreciate the impermanence of all things.

Transformation is the culmination of love and loss. It is the phoenix rising from the ashes, the caterpillar becoming a butterfly. It is the constant evolution of our being, as we shed old layers of ourselves to make way for new growth. Embracing transformation means letting go of the past and stepping boldly into the future.

Life is a journey of continual embrace—a dance with complexity, love, loss, and transformation. As we move forward, let us carry with us the wisdom gained from our experiences, knowing that the path ahead is not always easy, but it is always worth traversing. With open hearts and minds, we can embrace the unknown, celebrate the beauty in life's intricacies, and find strength in the unending journey of love, loss, and transformation. Together, we can navigate the winding road ahead and create a future filled with meaning, purpose, and fulfillment.